Pickle in the Middle

Pickle in the Middle and other easy snacks

BY FRANCES ZWEIFEL

An I CAN READ Book

HARPER & ROW, PUBLISHERS
New York, Hagerstown, San Francisco, London

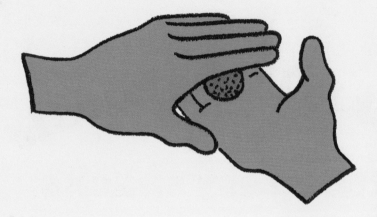

Library of Congress Cataloging in Publication Data
Zweifel, Frances W
    Pickle in the middle and other easy snacks.

    (An I can read book)
    SUMMARY: Presents simple, no-cook snacks.
    1. Cookery—Juvenile literature.   2. Snack
foods—Juvenile literature.   [1. Snack foods.
2. Cookery]   I. Title.
TX652.5.Z93   641.5'3   78-19478
ISBN 0-06-027072-1
ISBN 0-06-027073-X lib. bdg.

To Pat
Vivian
Monica
Margaret

Contents

Snacks for Your Sweet Tooth

Snacks to Drink

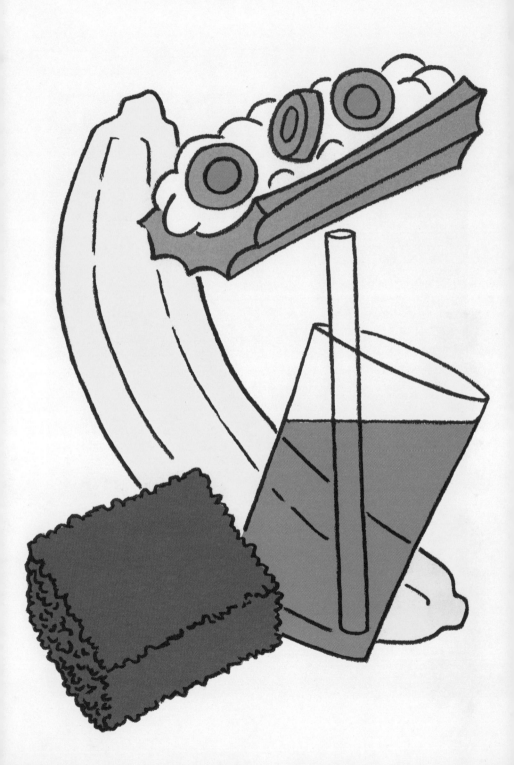

About This Book

You can use this cookbook by yourself.
You do not need a stove.
You do not need a sharp knife.

Your hands are your best tools.
You will pinch and squeeze
and crumble and pound the food.
To keep the food safe to eat,
your hands must be very clean.

Ask some friends to cook with you.
You will make good things to eat.
It is fun to cook,
and it is fun to eat what you cook!

How to Be a Good Cook

1. Read the recipe 2 times.
   The recipe tells you what to use
   and how to cook.

2. Get out the tools you will need.
   Make sure they are very clean.

3. Wash your hands.
   Do not touch your face or hair
   while you cook.

4. Get out the food you will need.

5. Follow the cooking steps
   one by one.

6. Clean up the kitchen so people
   will be happy when you cook again.

Ask for adult help if you need it.
If you make a mistake,
don't worry.
Some mistakes taste good!

Cooking Tools

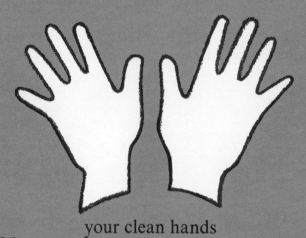

your clean hands

¼ teaspoon

½ teaspoon

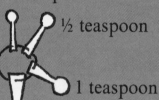

1 teaspoon

1 Tablespoon

measuring spoons

measuring cups

big mixing spoon

baking pan

plastic bags

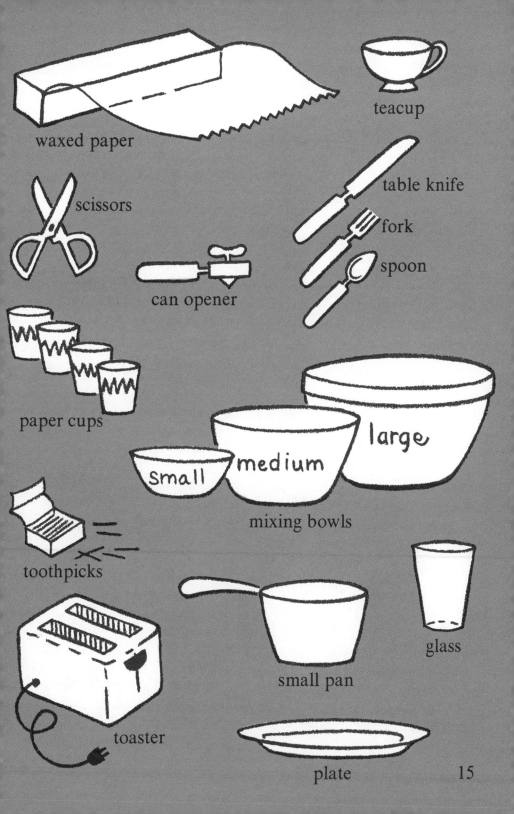

waxed paper

teacup

scissors

can opener

table knife

fork

spoon

paper cups

small

medium

large

mixing bowls

toothpicks

small pan

glass

toaster

plate

15

How to Measure

WET things like honey, milk, and juice:

Fill the measuring spoon
or cup to the top.

DRY things like cereal, powdered milk,
sugar, and cocoa:

Fill the measuring spoon
or cup over the top.
Then scrape the
extra food
off the top.
Make it level.

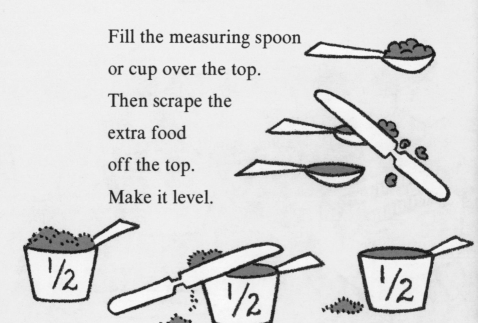

How to Open a Can Safely

Cut all the way around the top of the can with the can opener.

Lift the lid with the fork. Do not lift the sharp lid with your fingers.

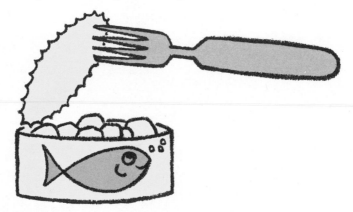

Carefully throw the lid away.

Fruit Spears

10 spears

1 small can of pineapple chunks

1 banana

10 strawberries

1. Open the can of pineapple chunks
   (first read page 17).
   Put 10 chunks on the plate.

2. Peel the banana.
   Cut it into
   10 pieces.
   Put them
   on the plate.

3. Wash the strawberries.

   Take the green stems off.

4. Spear a toothpick through a strawberry.

   Then spear the same toothpick

   through a pineapple chunk.

   Then spear the same

   toothpick into

   a piece of banana.

5. Use up all the fruit.

   Put the Fruit Spears on the plate.

   Pass the plate to your friends.

You can use grapes instead of strawberries.
Take out the grape seeds first.

19

Cinnamon Toast

2 pieces

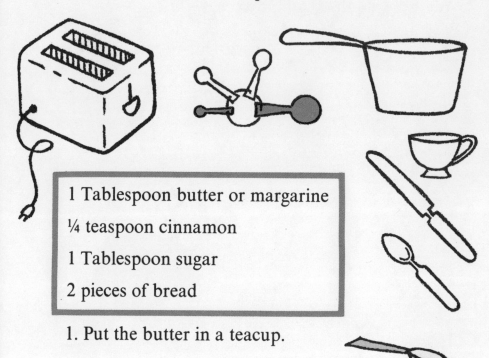

1 Tablespoon butter or margarine

¼ teaspoon cinnamon

1 Tablespoon sugar

2 pieces of bread

1. Put the butter in a teacup.

2. Run some hot water from the faucet
   into the pan. Set the teacup in the pan
   of hot water. Stir the butter
   until it gets soft.

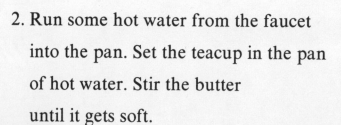

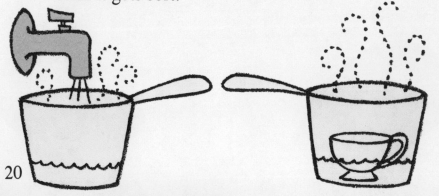

3. Add the cinnamon and the sugar
   to the soft butter.
   Stir until
   the mixture
   is creamy.

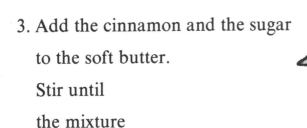

4. Toast the bread.

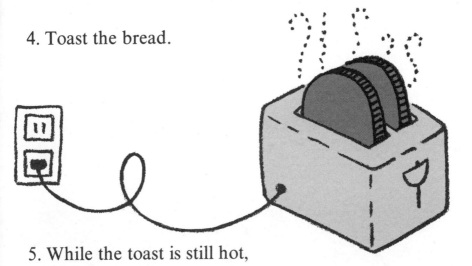

5. While the toast is still hot,
   spread half the butter mixture
   on each piece.

Yogurt Fruit Crunch Lunch

1 serving

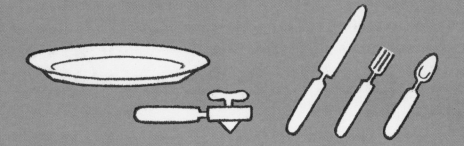

1 lettuce leaf

1 banana

½ container of fruit yogurt,
    such as blueberry or strawberry

Some crisp Chinese noodles from a can

1. Wash the lettuce leaf in cold water.
   Shake it off. Put it on the plate.

2. Peel the banana. Cut it up.
   Put the pieces on
   the lettuce.

3. Stir the yogurt. Spoon
   some yogurt on the
   banana pieces.

4. Open the can of Chinese noodles
   (first read page 17).
   Sprinkle some noodles on the yogurt.

You can use a pear or a peach
instead of a banana.
You can use salted peanuts
instead of noodles. YUM!

Tuna Cottage

enough for 4

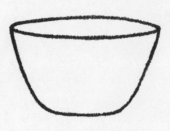

1 can chunky tuna (7 ounces)

1 sweet pickle

½ cup cottage cheese

Crackers or celery sticks

1. Open the can of tuna (first read page 17). Put the tuna in the medium bowl.

2. Cut the pickle into tiny pieces with scissors. Put the pieces in the bowl.

3. Put the cottage cheese in the bowl with the tuna and pickle. Mix.

4. Wash the celery in cold water. Cut off the leaves.

5. Put some Tuna Cottage on the celery sticks or crackers.

Keep leftover Tuna Cottage in the refrigerator.

Honey Fruit Cups

4 servings

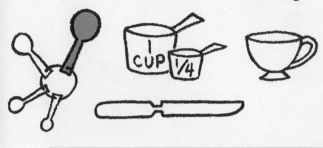

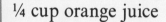

¼ cup orange juice

1 Tablespoon honey

1 apple, 1 orange, and 1 banana

1 cup grapes or berries

1. Mix the orange juice and the honey
   in the teacup.

2. Wash the apple. Cut it into 4 parts.
   Cut away the core and the seeds.
   Cut the apple into bite-size pieces.
   Put the pieces in the large bowl.

3. Pour the orange juice and honey
   over the apple pieces. Mix gently.

4. Peel the orange. Pull it apart.
   Take out the seeds.
   Put the pieces in the bowl.

5. Peel the banana. Cut it up.
   Put the pieces in the bowl.

6. Wash the grapes or berries.
   Pour them in the bowl.

7. Mix gently. Spoon it into 4 paper cups.

Try this—banana and pineapple
and strawberries together. YUM!

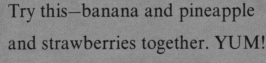

Bright-Eyes Cream Cheese
enough for 3

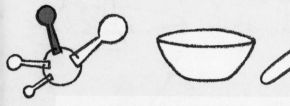

1 small package of cream cheese (3 ounces)

1 teaspoon olive juice

16 small stuffed olives

Crackers or celery sticks

1. Put the cream cheese in the small bowl.
   Mash the cheese with the spoon.
   Mix it until it gets soft.

2. Take a teaspoon of juice from the
   olive jar. Pour it on the cream cheese.
   Mix until the cheese
   is smooth.

3. With the scissors, cut the stuffed olives into slices.

4. Put the olive slices in the cream cheese. Mix gently.

5. Wash the celery in cold water. Cut off the leaves.

6. Put some Bright-Eyes Cream Cheese on the crackers or celery sticks.

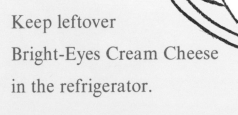

Keep leftover
Bright-Eyes Cream Cheese
in the refrigerator.

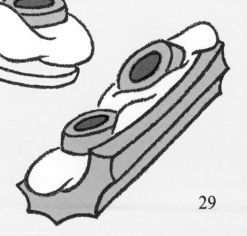

Bologna Roll-Ups

2 servings

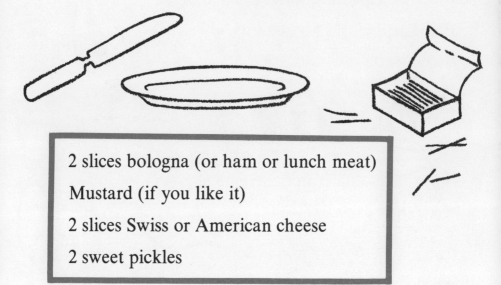

2 slices bologna (or ham or lunch meat)

Mustard (if you like it)

2 slices Swiss or American cheese

2 sweet pickles

1. Put a slice of bologna on the plate.

   If you like mustard,

   spread some on the bologna.

2. Put a slice of cheese
   on the bologna.

3. Cut a pickle in half the long way.
   Put the 2 pickle halves on the cheese,
   end to end.

4. Roll up the bologna and cheese
   around the pickle.
   Stick toothpicks in the Roll-Up
   to hold it together.

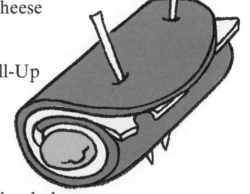

5. Do steps 1 to 4 with the other bologna
   and cheese and pickle.

Eat your Roll-Ups like hot dogs.
But don't eat the toothpicks!

Crunchy Banana

1 serving

1 banana

2 or 3 graham crackers

Milk

1. Peel the banana. Cut it up.

   Put the pieces in the small bowl.

2. Mash the banana with the fork.

3. Crumble 2 graham crackers
   over the mashed banana.
   If you like more crunch,
   crumble 1 more
   graham cracker.

4. Pour milk into the bowl.
   Stir gently with the spoon.

This snack makes a good breakfast.

Pickle in the Middle

about 20 spears

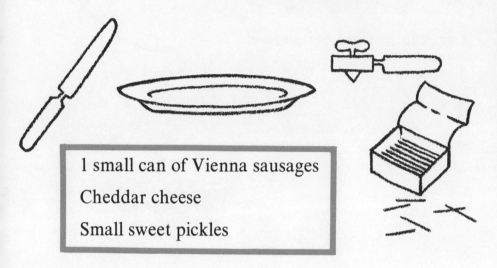

1 small can of Vienna sausages

Cheddar cheese

Small sweet pickles

1. Open the can of sausages
   (first read page 17). Pour off the juice.
   Put the sausages on the plate.

2. Cut each sausage into 3 pieces.
   Count the pieces.

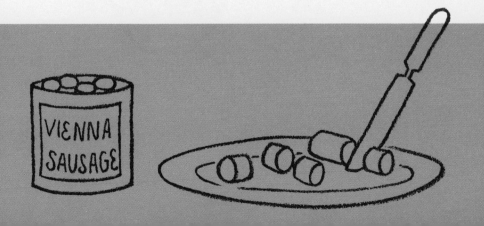

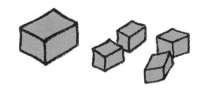

3. Cut small squares of cheese.

   Cut one square for each piece of sausage.

4. Cut the pickles into bite-size pieces.

   Cut one piece for each piece of sausage.

5. Push a toothpick through a sausage piece.

   Then push the same toothpick through a

   piece of pickle.

   Then push the same

   toothpick into

   a square of cheese.

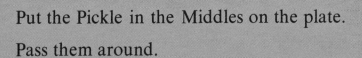

Put the Pickle in the Middles on the plate.

Pass them around.

Buttered Bites

enough for 8

½ stick of butter or margarine

3 cups bite-size, nonsweetened dry cereal

    (such as Wheat Chex or Corn Chex)

1 cup Cheerios

1 cup crisp Chinese noodles from a can

1. Cut the butter into pieces. Put them in the teacup.

2. Run some hot water from the faucet into the pan. Set the teacup in the pan of hot water to melt the butter.

3. If the water in the pan gets cool,
pour it out and put some more hot water in.
Do this until the butter is melted and runny.
Stir the butter to help it melt.

4. Put the bite-size cereal
and the Cheerios in the large bowl.

5. Open the can of Chinese noodles
(first read page 17).
Put the noodles in the bowl.

6. Mix the cereals and noodles with your hands.

7. Pour the melted butter into the bowl.
Mix with the big spoon
until all the pieces are buttered.

Eat Buttered Bites like popcorn.

Apple Devil

enough for 4

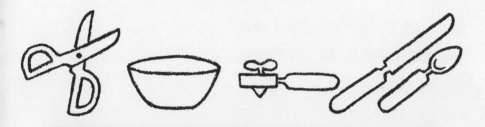

> 1 small can of deviled ham or deviled Spam
>
> 1 small jar of pimiento cheese spread
>
> 1 or 2 small sweet pickles
>
> 2 apples

1. Open the can of deviled ham (first read page 17). Put the deviled ham into the small bowl.

2. Open the jar of cheese spread. Put the cheese in the bowl with the deviled ham. Mix together.

3. Cut the pickles into tiny pieces
   with the scissors. Put the pieces
   into the bowl.
   Mix again.

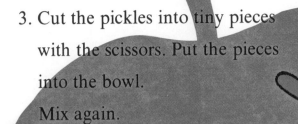

4. Wash the apples. Cut each apple into
   4 parts. Cut away the core and seeds.
   Cut the apple pieces into slices.

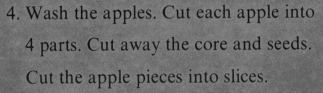

5. Spread the cheese and ham mixture
   on the apple slices.

Keep leftover Apple Devil
in the refrigerator.

Chocolate Peanut Toast Sticks

2 servings

Chocolate sprinkles
2 pieces of bread
Peanut butter

1. Put some chocolate sprinkles in the small bowl.

2. Cut the crusts from the bread.

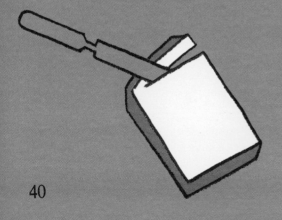

3. Toast the bread.
   Make the toast crisp.
   Soft toast
   will not work.

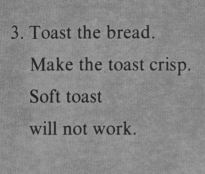

4. Cut each piece of toast
   into 4 long sticks.

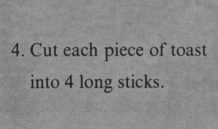

5. Spread peanut butter on
   the 4 long sides
   of each stick.

6. Roll each stick in
   the chocolate sprinkles.
   Put the sticks on the plate.

Apricot Nips

20 sweets

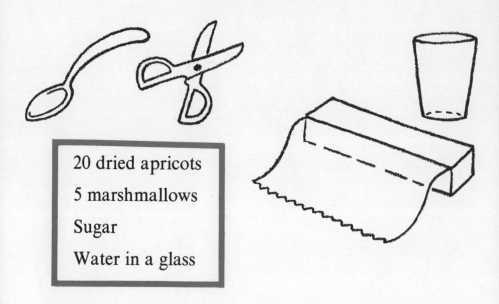

20 dried apricots

5 marshmallows

Sugar

Water in a glass

1. Put a sheet of waxed paper on the table.
   Sprinkle some sugar on the paper.

2. Put 4 dried apricots
   on the paper. Spread
   the apricots flat.
   Sprinkle a little
   more sugar
   on the apricots.

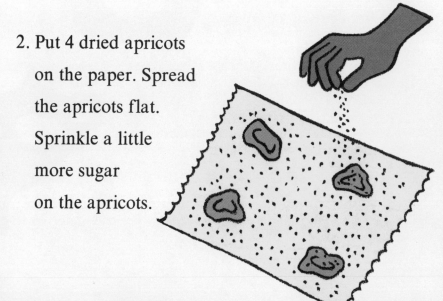

3. Put another sheet of waxed paper over the apricots. Pound the apricots with the big spoon until they are thin and flat. Peel off the top waxed paper.

4. Cut a marshmallow into 4 parts. If the scissors get sticky, dip them in water.

5. Put a piece of marshmallow on each flat apricot.
   Fold the apricot around the marshmallow piece.
   Pinch the apricot closed.

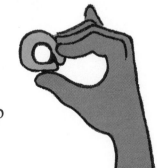

6. Do steps 1 to 5 again, until you use up all the apricots and marshmallows.

Honey Fruit Peanut Butter Balls

about 24 balls

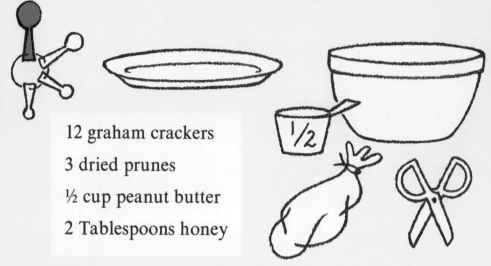

12 graham crackers

3 dried prunes

½ cup peanut butter

2 Tablespoons honey

1. Put 6 graham crackers into the plastic bag. Press the bag flat. Tie it closed. Whack the crackers with the big spoon until they are very fine crumbs.

2. Put the crumbs into the large bowl.

3. Whack all the crackers into crumbs.

4. With the scissors, cut the prunes into
   tiny pieces. Mix them with the crumbs.

5. Put the peanut butter and the honey into
   the bowl. Mix everything with the spoon.

6. With your hands, squeeze the mixture
   until it sticks together.

7. Take out a big pinch of the mixture.
   Roll it into a ball in your hands.
   Put the ball
   on the plate.

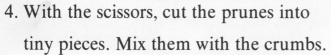

8. Repeat step 7 until you use up
   all the mixture.

9. Let the Honey Fruit Peanut Butter Balls
   rest for 10 minutes before you eat them.

Candy Blips

about 30 pieces

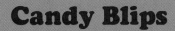

⅓ cup powdered sugar

⅓ cup honey

⅓ cup crunchy peanut butter

½ cup powdered skim milk

more powdered sugar

1. Measure the powdered sugar
   and put it into the teacup.

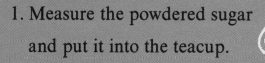

2. Pour the honey into the large bowl.

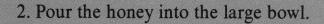

3. Use the same measuring cup for the
   peanut butter. Put the peanut butter into
   the bowl with the honey. Mix well.

4. Put the powdered milk and powdered sugar into the bowl. Mix again.

5. Use your hands to mix and squeeze the candy until it sticks together in a ball.

6. Put a sheet of waxed paper on the table. Sprinkle some powdered sugar on it. Put half the candy on the paper. Roll the candy into a sausage.

7. Do the same with the other half of the candy. Put the rolls in a cool place for 15 minutes.

8. Cut the candy rolls into bite-size pieces.

Wrap leftover pieces in waxed paper. Keep them in the refrigerator.

Creamy Dates

about 30 sweets

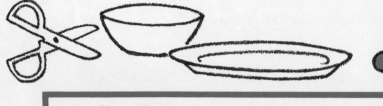

1 small package of cream cheese (3 ounces)

4 teaspoons sugar

1 teaspoon orange juice

1 package of dates

1. Put the cream cheese in the small bowl.

   Mash the cheese with the spoon.

   Mix it until it gets soft.

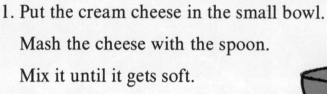

2. Sprinkle the sugar on the cream cheese.

3. Pour the orange juice on the cheese.

4. Mix the cheese and sugar and juice

   until it is all creamy and smooth.

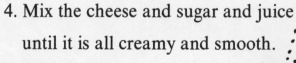

5. Cut open a date on one side.
   If there is a seed, take it out.

6. Spread the date open
   on the plate.

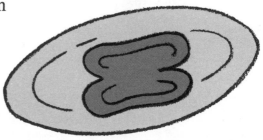

7. Put some cream cheese mixture on one
   half of the date. Fold the date closed.

8. Do steps 5, 6, and 7 until you use up
   all the dates.

Keep leftover Creamy Dates in the refrigerator.

Orange Balls

about 30 cookies

60 round vanilla wafers, or about 5½ oz.

¼ cup orange juice

4 teaspoons honey

Sugar

1. Put 10 vanilla wafers in a plastic bag.

   Press the bag flat.

   Tie it closed.

   Whack the bag with the big spoon until
   all the wafers are tiny crumbs.

2. Pour the crumbs into the medium bowl.

3. Do this with all the wafers.

4. Pour the orange juice into the bowl.
   Mix with the fork
   until it looks like wet sand.

5. Put the honey in the bowl. Mix and mash
   with the fork until it sticks together.

6. Put some sugar in the small bowl.

7. Pinch off a piece of the mixture.
   Roll it into a ball.
   The ball should be as big
   as an acorn or a marble.

8. Roll the ball in the sugar.
   Put it on the plate.
   Make more Orange Balls.

   Let the Orange Balls rest for 10 minutes.

Sticky Stuff
4 servings

8 dates

⅓ cup raisins

8 walnut halves

1 cup nonsweetened bite-size whole wheat
    cereal (such as Wheat Chex)

4 teaspoons honey

1. Cut the dates into tiny pieces.
Put the pieces in the
medium bowl.

2. Cut each raisin in half.
Put the pieces in the bowl.

3. Cut the walnut halves into small
   pieces. Put them in the bowl.

4. Crumble the dry cereal with your
   hands. Put the crumbs in the bowl.

5. Pour the honey
   over the crumbs
   in the bowl.
   Mix with the spoon.

6. Spoon Sticky Stuff into 4 paper cups.
   Put the cups in a cool place for at least
   15 minutes. Eat it with a spoon.

Sticky Stuff tastes even better
if you let it cool longer.

Raisin Bars

16 bar cookies

16 graham crackers

1 can sweetened condensed milk

1 cup raisins

2 cups nonsweetened dry cereal (like crisp
   rice or corn flakes or wheat flakes)

Some butter or margarine

1. Put 4 graham crackers in the plastic
   bag. Press the bag flat. Tie it closed.
   Whack the crackers with the big spoon
   until they are tiny crumbs.

2. Put the crumbs in the large bowl.
   Whack all the crackers into crumbs.

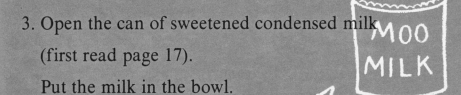

3. Open the can of sweetened condensed milk (first read page 17).
   Put the milk in the bowl.

4. Put the raisins in the bowl.
   Mix with the big spoon.

5. Add the cereal to the bowl.
   Mix. It will be stiff. You
   may have to use your hands.

6. Spread some butter all over the inside
   of the baking pan.

7. Put the mixture in the pan.
   Press it down with your fingers.

8. Let the pan sit for 15 minutes.
   Cut the mixture into 16 bars.

Chocolate Lumps

about 25 cookies

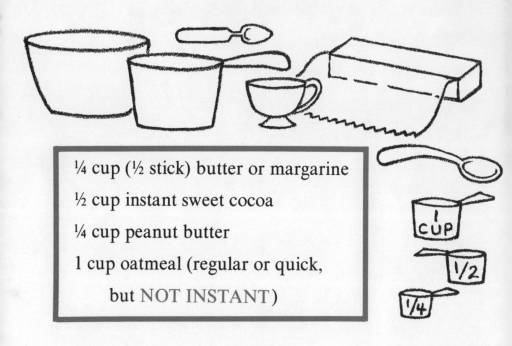

¼ cup (½ stick) butter or margarine

½ cup instant sweet cocoa

¼ cup peanut butter

1 cup oatmeal (regular or quick,

but NOT INSTANT)

1. Put the butter in the teacup.

2. Run some hot water from the faucet
   into the pan. Set the teacup in the pan
   of hot water to melt the butter.
   If the water in the pan gets cool,
   pour it out. Put more hot water in the
   pan. Stir the butter to help it melt.

3. Pour the melted butter into the medium bowl. Add the instant cocoa. Mix together.

4. Add the peanut butter to the bowl. Mix until it is smooth.

5. Put the oatmeal in the bowl. Mix well.

6. Put a sheet of waxed paper on the table.

7. Take a small spoonful of the chocolate mixture. Put it on the waxed paper. Do this until all the mixture is used up.

8. Let the cookies rest in a cool place for 10 minutes.

Brown Sugar Bumps

about 25 cookies

¼ cup (½ stick) butter or margarine

½ cup brown sugar

¼ cup peanut butter

1 cup oatmeal (regular or quick,

  but NOT INSTANT)

1. Put the butter in the teacup.

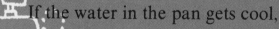

2. Run some hot water from the faucet
   into the pan. Set the teacup in the pan
   of hot water to melt the butter.
   If the water in the pan gets cool,
   pour it out. Put more hot water in the
   pan. Stir the butter to help it melt.

3. Pour the melted butter into the large bowl.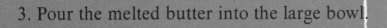

4. Pack the ½-cup measure with brown sugar.
   Put the sugar in the bowl. Mix.

5. Put the peanut butter in the bowl. Mix.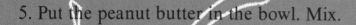

6. Put the oatmeal in the bowl. Mix well.

7. Put a sheet of waxed paper on the table.

8. Put a small spoonful of the cookie mix
   on the waxed paper. Gently pinch it
   to make it round.
   Do the same
   with the rest of the mix.

9. Let the Brown Sugar Bumps rest in a
   cool place for 15 minutes or more.

Eggnog

1 serving

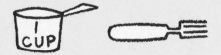

1 egg

1 cup cold milk

½ teaspoon vanilla

2 teaspoons sugar or honey

1. Crack the egg on the edge of the pan.

   Pull the shell apart

   and let the egg fall into the pan.

   Beat it with the fork until it is foamy.

2. Pour the milk and vanilla and sugar

   into the pan. Beat well.

3. Pour the eggnog into the glass.

Warm Spice Cocoa

1 serving

¼ cup powdered skim milk

A pinch of cinnamon

2 Tablespoons instant cocoa mix

Very hot water from the faucet

1. Put the powdered milk, the cinnamon, and the cocoa mix in the teacup.

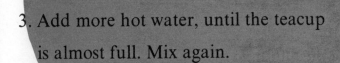

2. Put a little hot water in the cup. Mix slowly.

3. Add more hot water, until the teacup is almost full. Mix again.

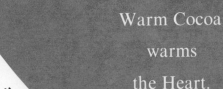

Warm Cocoa

warms

the Heart.

Pink Lemonade

1 serving

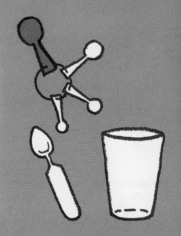

Cold water

2 Tablespoons lemon juice

1 Tablespoon sugar or honey

Cranberry juice

3 ice cubes

1. Fill the glass half full of cold water.

2. Put the lemon juice and sugar into the glass. Stir slowly.

3. Put 3 ice cubes in the glass.

4. Slowly pour cranberry juice into the glass until it is almost full. Stir again.

Grape Fizzle

1 serving

3 ice cubes

A piece of lemon

Ginger ale

Grape juice

1. Put 3 ice cubes into the glass.

2. Squeeze the piece
   of lemon into the glass.

3. Fill the glass half full of ginger ale.

4. Slowly pour grape juice
   into the glass until
   it is almost full.

Orange Nog
1 serving

  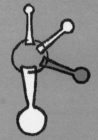 

¼ cup orange juice

1 teaspoon sugar

2 ice cubes

Cold milk

1. Put the orange juice and the sugar
   into the glass. Mix together.

2. Put 2 ice cubes in the glass.

3. Slowly pour milk
   into the glass
   until it is
   almost full.
   Mix again.